Benjamin Franklin

Thinker, Inventor, Leader

Jeanne Dustman

Consultant

Glenn Manns, M.A.
Teaching American History Coordinator
Ohio Valley Educational Cooperative

Publishing Credits

Dona Herweck Rice, *Editor-in-Chief*; Lee Aucoin, *Creative Director*; Conni Medina, M.A.Ed., *Editorial Director*; Jamey Acosta, *Associate Editor*; Neri Garcia, *Senior Designer*; Stephanie Reid, *Photo Researcher*; Rachelle Cracchiolo, M.A.Ed., *Publisher*

Teacher Created Materials

5301 Oceanus Drive
Huntington Beach, CA 92649-1030
http://www.tcmpub.com
ISBN 978-1-4333-1600-5
©2011 Teacher Created Materials, Inc.
Printed in China

Table of Contents

Growing Up

Benjamin Franklin was born in 1706. He lived in Boston, Massachusetts (mas-uh-CHOO-sits). He had nine brothers and seven sisters.

Young Ben selling poems on the streets of Boston

Ben's home in Boston

Long ago, most boys went to work when they were young. Ben only went to school for one year. He liked to read and write.

Fun Fact

Children read from hornbooks. Hornbooks were wooden paddles with words on them.

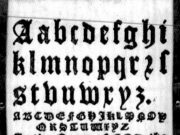

Ben worked at his father's candle shop.

This picture shows how candles were made.

Ben did not like making candles. He went to work at his brother's print shop. One of his jobs was to print money. Soon Ben started his own print shop.

Ben outside his print shop

Ben the printer

New Ideas

Ben was an **inventor**. He had many good ideas. Ben worked hard to make his ideas come true. He started the first fire department in America. Ben started the first police force in Philadelphia (fill-uh-DEL-fee-uh), too.

An American fire engine from 1760

A police officer from the early 1900s

Fun Fact

Ben started the first street cleaning service, too.

Back then, books cost a lot of money. Most people did not own books. Ben and some friends opened a **library**. It was the first library in America. People could **borrow** books from the library.

Ben's library in Philadelphia

Ben inside the first library

Many Americans were poor. They needed help when they got sick. Ben and a friend started a **hospital**. At the hospital, doctors helped sick people get better.

Fun Fact

The hospital Ben started is still open today.

Ben's hospital

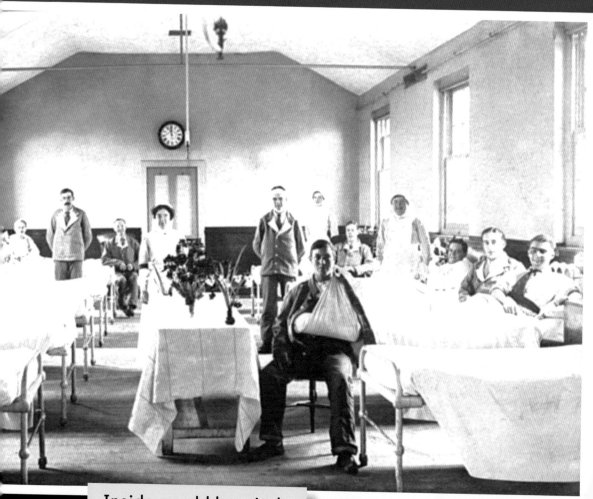

Inside an old hospital

Long ago, it was hard to send letters to people who lived far away. Ben started a new mail service. He was the first **postmaster** in Philadelphia.

A Benjamin Franklin postage stamp

A postwoman from 1916

A motorcycle postman from 1912

Inventor

Ben was **curious**. He put a key on a kite string. Lightning hit Ben's key. He got a shock. He found out that lightning is **electricity** (ee-lek-TRIS-ih-tee).

Ben and his son complete their experiment with a kite and key.

Lightning strikes!

Winters were cold. People needed heat. Ben the inventor made a new stove. It was cleaner than a fireplace. It made more heat, too.

A man using Ben's stove

A wood-burning stove

Leader

Ben helped write the **Declaration** (dek-luh-RAY-shuhn) **of Independence** (in-di-PEN-duhns). This letter said that America was free from Great Britain (BRIT-en). Great Britain did not want America to be free. A war started between the two countries.

Declaration of Independence

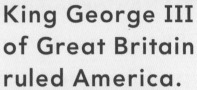

King George III of Great Britain ruled America.

King George III

A map of the 13 colonies

America was losing the war. Ben met with the king of France. Ben asked the king to help America. France sent money and soldiers. They helped America beat Great Britain.

Ben at an important meeting

Ben at a party in France

America won the war. Ben was good at working with others. He worked with British leaders to write a peace **treaty**. The treaty said that America was free.

Fun Fact

The red marks below are wax. Long ago, people put wax next to their names on important papers. They put their fingerprint in the wax.

The Treaty of Paris

Benjamin Franklin

THE LAST RESTING PLACE OF
BENJAMIN FRANKLIN
1706 — 1790

"VENERATED FOR BENEVOLENCE.
ADMIRED FOR TALENTS. ESTEEMED
FOR PATRIOTISM. BELOVED FOR
PHILANTHROPY."

WASHINGTON

"THE SAGE WHOM TWO WORLDS
CLAIMED AS THEIR OWN."

MIRABEAU

"HE TORE FROM THE SKIES THE
LIGHTNING AND FROM TYRANTS
THE SCEPTRE."

TURGOT

Ben died on April 17, 1790. He was 84.

1706	1728	1737
Ben Franklin is born in Boston, Massachusetts.	Ben starts his own print shop.	Ben becomes the first postmaster in Philadelphia.

Line

1752

Ben becomes an inventor.

1776

Ben helps write the Declaration of Independence.

1790

Ben dies at the age of 84.

Glossary

borrow—to use something that belongs to someone else, such as a library book

Declaration of Independence—a paper people wrote to say that the 13 American colonies were free from Great Britain

electricity—a type of energy that travels through wires and makes things such as lights work

hospital—a place where sick or hurt people go to get better

inventor—a person who makes something new and different

library—a place that has books to read or borrow

postmaster—a person in charge of a post office

treaty—a formal agreement between two or more states or countries

Index

Americans Today

Dr. Patricia Bath is the first African American woman to create medical inventions. Her inventions have helped blind people see!